BOA
EDITION
LIMITED

The Boatloads

by Dan Albergotti

Winner, 2007 A. Poulin, Jr. Poetry Prize

Selected by Edward Hirsch

The Boatloads

by Dan Albergotti

Foreword by Edward Hirsch

A. Poulin, Jr. New Poets of America Series, No. 30

BOA Editions, Ltd. • Rochester, NY • 2008

First Edition
08 09 10 11 7 6 5 4 3 2 1

For information about permission to reuse any material from this book please contact
The Permissions Company at www.permissionscompany.com or e-mail permdude@
eclipse.net

Publications and programs by BOA Editions, Ltd. – a not-for-profit corporation
under section 501 (c)(3) of the United States Internal Revenue Code – are made
possible with the assistance of grants from the Literature Program of the New York
State Council on the Arts; the Literature Program of the National Endowment for the
Arts; the County of Monroe, NY; the Lannan Foundation for support of the Lannan
Translations Selection Series; the Sonia Raiziss Giop Charitable Foundation; the Mary
S. Mulligan Charitable Trust; the Rochester Area Community Foundation; the Arts
& Cultural Council for Greater Rochester; the Steeple-Jack Fund; the Ames Amzalak
Memorial Trust in memory of Henry Ames, Semon Amzalak and Dan Amzalak; the
TCA Foundation; and contributions from many individuals nationwide. See Colophon
on page 96 for special individual acknowledgements.

Cover Design: Geri McCormick
Cover Art: "Chairs" by Anne Havens
Interior Design and Composition: Scott McCarney
Manufacturing: Thomson-Shore
BOA Logo: Mirko

LIBRARY OF CONGRESS CATALOGING-IN-PUBLICATION DATA

Albergotti, Dan.
The boatloads / by Dan Albergotti. — 1st ed.
    p. cm. — (New poets of America series; no. 30)
Includes bibliographical references.
ISBN 978-1-934414-03-3 (alk. paper)
    I. Title.
PS3601.L3343B63 2008
813'.6 — dc22   2007039112

BOA Editions, Ltd.
Nora A. Jones, Executive Director/Publisher
Thom Ward, Editor/Production
Peter Conners, Editor/Marketing
A. Poulin, Jr., President (1938–1996)
250 N. Goodman Street, Suite 306
Rochester, NY 14607
www.boaeditions.org

State of the Arts

NYSCA

NATIONAL
ENDOWMENT
FOR THE ARTS

Have mercy upon us. O Lord, have mercy upon us:
for we are exceedingly filled with contempt.
—Psalm 123

Contents

III

Foreword

Dan Albergotti's first book, *The Boatloads*, is filled with the spirit of mystery. It begins in wonder and ends in awe. Albergotti is a poet of deep conviction, a rare quality in our cynical times. He is a genuine seeker, a man on a spiritual quest, a stubborn questioner, and his poems are infused with the sense that the earth itself is sacred. Longing for a world beyond ourselves, he ventures forth without the consolations of belief. "I do not believe a special providence / makes this world say anything," he confesses in one poem. "*Oh my lord, my absent God*," he laments in another. He is a restless searcher who keeps bumping up against the void.

The Boatloads begins with an irreverent sexual anecdote, a memory. A man recalls how he and his girlfriend—two mischievous teenagers—once snuck into a university chapel and made love. What is striking about this prefatory poem, "Vestibule," is how it overcomes its boyish irony, its braggadocio ("Where's the strangest place you've ever…?") and turns into a secular lyric that rescues a bedrock truth "that the heart is holy even when / our own hearts were so frail and callow." What compels is the attitude it develops, a kind of gutsy insouciance, a determination to take something potentially tawdry and name it in high religious terms. The erotic incident takes on the language of a hymn. You may be skeptical, he suggests, but he is sticking to experience, to what he knows.

> Truth: it was 1983; we were nineteen years old;
> we lay below the altar and preached a quiet sermon
> not just on the divinity of skin, but on the grace
> of the heart beneath. It was the only homily
> we knew, and our souls were beatified.
> And if you say sentiment and cliché, then that
> is what you say. What I know is what is sacred.

There is a liturgical element to *The Boatloads*, a series of repeated patterns and obsessions. The ground note is established in the strange epigraph from Psalm 123: "Have mercy upon us. O Lord, have mercy upon us: for we are exceedingly filled with contempt." How to transcend human contempt, a world we repeatedly degrade, is one of the recurrent questions of this tripartite book. "We want to find higher intent, a god to damn," he writes in "Rhetoric": "*But not so.*" We are left to our own devices.

Albergotti writes in a vernacular idiom—there is nothing here that a contemporary speaker wouldn't *say*—but he harnesses power from biblical texts, which haunt him. His poems tend to develop around anecdotes, which he narrates with a sly playfulness, but they reach for a prophetic note. The opening of "Dark Laughter" is characteristic:

> *There's nothing funny about this,* she said,
> but that only made me laugh harder. I wish
> I could have said that inappropriate laughter
> is the most human, as is open weeping
> after the best sex. *Excess of sorrow laughs,*
> said William Blake. *Excess of joy weeps.*

The quest for the sacred, which is always haunted by death, is one of the determining features of this collection. There are lyrics the poet calls "prayers," others he deems "lessons." There are strategically placed lessons, for example, for each of the four elements. There are two songs of the gods, which is to say poems that take a viewpoint beyond the human fray, plus a third entitled "The Last Song of the One True God" ("the song none of us will ever hear"). There are poems that hark back to Adam ("The Age of Adam") and the great Flood ("When the World Was Only Ocean"). One is called "Book of the Father," another "Corinthians." Albergotti likes parabolic structure and creates his own wry religious parables, as in "Day Eight."

> The lord is embarrassed. He realizes
> only now that he will have to inhabit
> the world he has made. He will be made
> to endure the praises of the thinking creatures
> and the indifference of the beautiful ones.
> It's going to be hell. It's going to be
> day after day of regret and chagrin.
> And he wishes he had not made the son
> a sacrificial lamb. He wishes he had not
> made the daughter's hair auburn.
> He wishes he had not left so many questions.
> He almost wants to apologize for the mosquito.
> It's only morning, but it already feels
> like a long day. He's already thinking about the rain.

God is deflated here. Like us, he is forced to inhabit and endure the fallen world.

These poems keep circling certain subjects, which they can't let go. One is the mystery of an elemental nature that defies the names we give to it. "The poet tries to make the heron a god, / but the heron does not care," one poem begins. Another is the struggle to come to terms with an incomprehensible human cruelty: "What song could be in the filthy basement / where the small boy is chained to a beam, / his mouth gagged with an athletic sock?" Albergotti won't let us forget that horrific song in the basement. We are left to ourselves, to what we call human nature. So, too, we are left to ponder a silent Lord who has apparently turned His back on us. He is palpably absent.

Albergotti also balances these dark truths with an abiding,

equally powerful sense of gratitude. He likes catalogs of unlikely pleasures. One of my favorite poems is a list entitled, "Among the Things He Does Not Deserve."

> Greek olives in oil, fine beer, the respect of colleagues,
> the rapt attention of an audience, pressed white shirts,
> just one last-second victory, sympathy, buttons made
> to resemble pearls, a pale daughter, living wages, a father
> with Italian blood, pity, the miraculous reversal of time,
> a benevolent god, good health, another dog, nothing
> cruel and unusual, spring, forgiveness, the benefit
> of the doubt, the next line, cold fingers against his chest,
> rich bass notes from walnut speakers, inebriation, more ink,
> a hanging curve, great art, steady rain on Sunday, the purr
> of a young cat, the crab cakes at their favorite little place,
> the dull pain in his head, the soft gift of her parted lips.

I like the way this tribute poem—a sentence fragment—contains small details (pressed white shirts) and large impossibilities (the miraculous reversal of time). It puts together a benevolent god, good health, and another dog all on the same line. It holds fast to—it treasures—the transient world.

So many of these images are shot through with a sense of preciousness in the face of death, which is one of the inescapable driving forces of lyric poetry. *The Boatloads* is everywhere death-haunted. The first section begins with "The Chiming of the Hour," a powerful poem about a widow that concludes, "Sometimes she wakes up singing." There is a recurrent sense here that God "sowed deep that hard seed / of death" ("Testimony"), that "The dead and dying sing a silent song" ("Song 378"). One of the strongest poems is a short enraged Eliotic catalog entitled "What Else Means Death." The penultimate poem fantasizes another life—a different end—for John Keats ("Revision"). The book concludes with the

Dantescan title poem, "The Boatloads," which begins: "Dante had not thought death had undone so many. / He had not been paying attention." Charon can barely keep up with all the people—person after person, too many to count—being hauled off.

> In the end, Charon must abandon formality,
> must drop the roll, extend his bony finger
> toward the crowd, and begin counting off,
> *you and you*, and *you and you and you.*

It is in the face of this anonymity, this endless lineup, that people must make meaning out of their lives. For this poet, for poetry itself, death is the mother of beauty, as Wallace Stevens said. The poems in Dan Albergotti's haunting first book are tributes rescued from oblivion. They begin in wonder and end in awe.

— Edward Hirsch

Vestibule

I sometimes wish I could find Cindy
to thank her for agreeing with my fine idea
that we sneak into the university chapel
late one night in 1983 to make love.
I don't just want to thank her for giving me
the trump card—"house of worship"—
I hold in every stupid party game that begins,
"Where's the strangest place you've ever…?"
No, I want to thank her for the truth of it.
For knowing that the heart is holy even when
our own hearts were so frail and callow.
Truth: it was 1983; we were nineteen years old;
we lay below the altar and preached a quiet sermon
not just on the divinity of skin, but on the grace
of the heart beneath. It was the only homily
we knew, and our souls were beatified.
And if you say sentiment and cliché, then that
is what you say. What I know is what is sacred.
Lord of this other world, let me recall that night.
Let me again hear how our whispered exclamations
near the end seemed like rising hymnal rhythm,
and let me feel how those forgotten words came
from somewhere else and meant something.
Something, if only to the single moth
that, in the darkened air of that chapel,
fluttered its dusty wings around our heads.

I

The Chiming of the Hour

The low tone of heavy December wind
moving through the attic's slatted vents
awakens the woman lying on her side.
She sees how the muted morning light
drifts through window blinds and how her husband,
who was alive in her dream, is again in the earth.
This is the gray day that the Lord hath made.
She hears the soft, rapid ticking of the clock
beside her bed and how it mingles with
the bells outside. The woman does not know
why the wind chimes sound altogether different
in winter months. She does not know
what puts her in her navy dress and heels,
behind the wheel of her husband's old sedan,
and into the pew they sat in all those years.
But she stands with the parishioners and mouths
the words of the doxology, her whisper lost
in the throng. She sits back down with them.
Back home, she will read the bulletin
and listen to the cable news anchorman
as if he were a bothersome neighbor child.
She does not know why she will not clean
the tables and mantelpiece of the gathering dust
nor why she has to check each windup clock
before she puts herself back into the dark.
Sometimes she wakes up singing.

Song of the Gods

We live in the light, unbeheld,
in morning glare and the low rays

of evening. Always here in the light.
And we are not seen. We are not seen

again. We do not grow old. Those who do
worship us. But they do not see us,

do not see that we are desire in the morning,
love in the afternoon, war as the light

grows weak. They only call us *desire,*
love, war, and everything. We are those sounds

insubstantial as words, that sudden thrill
in the veins. Everything that does not grow old.

We coil and uncoil like storm clouds,
moving in time but always in the light.

Those who die sing to us, but we
cannot sing back. The only song

is this song. Love in the morning,
war in the afternoon, desire as the light

fades. That light on the stone columns,
that light on the dial's face, that light

that lies across sand in silence, kicking up
flashes. War, desire, love as the light breaks.

And everything else unbeheld in the light.
Wisdom. Madness. Music. What else

do you hear in the song of the dying?
What else will make us live in the light?

Among the Things He Does Not Deserve

Greek olives in oil, fine beer, the respect of colleagues,
the rapt attention of an audience, pressed white shirts,
just one last-second victory, sympathy, buttons made
to resemble pearls, a pale daughter, living wages, a father
with Italian blood, pity, the miraculous reversal of time,
a benevolent god, good health, another dog, nothing
cruel and unusual, spring, forgiveness, the benefit
of the doubt, the next line, cold fingers against his chest,
rich bass notes from walnut speakers, inebriation, more ink,
a hanging curve, great art, steady rain on Sunday, the purr
of a young cat, the crab cakes at their favorite little place,
the dull pain in his head, the soft gift of her parted lips.

Affirmation of Faith

I believe there is nothing to be done
for the squirrel that's been dying
all morning on my gravel driveway.

Yet he refuses to stop moving his tail.
I believe that if I try to say nothing
the slow, steady movement of this world

will still say something. Like a squirrel falling
from a high limb with a graceless thud.
I believe in the father who could not feel

the world moving the day a sparrow
flew into the tall plate-glass window
of the living room. From his easy chair,

the father uttered the grunt of vague annoyance
and surprise he gives to all experience not routine.
I believe I stood and walked to the window

and watched the sparrow close her eyes
evenly over four minutes while her small head
became more and more perfectly framed

by an expanding halo of clear fluid. I believed then
that the halo would continue growing even
if a neighborhood cat were to spirit the carcass away,

that the night's forecast showers might spread
the bird's diluted life throughout the back yard.
"What are you *doing?*" my father finally blurted,

turning his annoyance on my silent vigil. "Nothing,"
I said to the back of his head and sat back down.
I do not believe my father can feel the movement.

I believe the squirrel's tail has stopped moving.
I do not believe a special providence
makes this world say anything. The squirrel is dead.

I believe nothing could be so very still.

Bad Language

We fear to speak, and silence coats the night air.
So we are dumb, as quiet as the kitchen pans
hanging on their cabinet hooks. What words
do we even have? The root of *fuck* is as much
to strike as *to copulate.* And sometimes *ravish*
is *to rape.* But when you're ravishing, you're
beautiful. Strikingly beautiful. Other tongues
do not help. Try saying "kiss me" on the streets
of Paris. God does not help. The Bible is full
of prohibition. *Thou shalt not,* saith the lord.
No sounds like *know. To know* is *to understand.*
In the Bible *to know* is *to fuck.* What do you mean
when you say *no*? I think I know. I want to know.
Understand me. You're ravishing. I want to know
you. Strike me. Don't leave me alone with self-
knowledge and these rich, fruitless, unspoken words.

A Prayer for My Daughter, Who Does Not Exist

Bless you, my hollow child, lying under nothing tonight
in one of those other worlds. Let there be wind, for there is
no wind. Let me hear it and fear nothing for you.

Bless your yawning, unreal mouth, your even breath.
When you wake, will your first word be *Daddy*
or *God*? Let it be *God*, let there be that.

Bless your tiny fingers playing on my face, in my hair,
under my skull. Let there be your soft touch, for there is
no touch. And let there be the light crescent moons of your nails.

Bless everything you will do and all your dreams.
Dream of your father. Dream of your god. Let there be
years and years and years, for there is no future.

And since between each world there is nothing,
let there be a prayer. Let me bless your too-pale skin,
your too-auburn hair, your beautiful impossibility.

The Osprey and the Late Afternoon

The fish glides in a thick world,
waving its body slowly forward
with thin pectorals, watching for glimmer,
for flashes of minnows, insects, hooks in the murk.

On this world's ceiling, sunlight undulates,
and the fish hovers up toward the surface,
feeding on these small lights until they
are swallowed in an expanding shadow.

.

My parents and I sit near the lake's bank
in lawn chairs, holding late afternoon drinks.
Light is fading, and my father is
enumerating the misfortunes of his friends.

"Everyone we know is in the hospital, it seems,"
he says. "That's what it's like when you get to be…"
But before he can finish, my mother
nearly throws herself out of her chair.

"Oh, look at that bird!" she says, and points to the sky,
her thin finger wagging urgently above her head.
Just beyond the bank, an osprey treads the air
with broad wings, holds a motionless flight.

We watch the fish eagle and imagine that she
is watching us too, not that her intent eyes
scan the water below, until she tucks her wings
in a fluid instant and becomes a stone in the air.

Her fall is the purest movement this day
could bear, something that bends time, enough
to make me think that the brief disturbance
of the surface is a water blossom I could pluck and save.

But the water settles, time moves, and we stand,
strain our eyes to follow the shrinking bird
that bears away a twisting burden. We are caught,
hooked in the eye by unseen talons, waiting for dark.

Lesson of the Elements: Air

Each time I went under,
I held the air in my lungs.

I was the drowning man.
I thought if I were to wash up

on the rocks like broken cargo
from a wreck, some god might breathe

new air into my lungs.
But I did not wash up.

I was an old man drowning
in his hospital room, going down

and down, the soft pumping sound
of air growing fainter.

I was the drowning man dreaming
of his first child, a daughter, and her

breath. In my drowning dream I saw
that when the baby does not breathe

at birth, you can make her breathe,
but when she does, you cannot

make her breathe the way you wish.
You cannot repair the damage

to her brain. You cannot stop
her steady descent into madness.

You cannot keep her from spitting out
in anger, hatred, or numb despair

every burning word of the air.

Thumbs

In your praise of the human body, give good verses
to the thumb, that glorious digit that allows us
to grip, to hold. Far too noble for the word *finger*.
Universal sign of approval. Absolutely essential
to the circle change. With what else could we dare
to offer figs to God? How foolish writing seems
without it. I could go on and on. But let this suffice:
My father's thumb once stood between a live tank shell
and a rock embedded in the ground he'd fallen to
at Fort Benning in 1945. That night the blood welled
under his nail, brought on nausea. He used the corner
of his razor to mine the center of that nail, working
until he struck a vital gusher, a spray of life freed
from his most human part, the essence of our being
soaring through the dark and still air of the barracks.

The Age of Adam

As historical record, the early chapters of Genesis are,
at best, spotty, passing over the most important details.
We have the idea, for instance, that Adam was created
an adult, but no age is registered. This glaring omission
creates a world of questions. Take hair, for example.
Was this man given the amount of hair one might grow
between infancy and adulthood? Or was he shorn?
What of the face? Was he formed clean-shaven? If so,
why? If not, why not? Pubic hair? No pubic hair?
And while we're in that region, how could the man
have even been given a working penis, if God, unsure
of the final product, had not yet decided upon Eve?

I have my own ideas. I say Adam was made eighteen
and God fashioned from his rib an attractive older woman—
say nineteen to twenty—with full, round breasts. I say
God gave her a tight, cream, v-neck sweater to insure
procreation. I say there must have been a '57 Chevy
parked somewhere in that lush garden, one with plenty
of leg room in the back. I say there are certain ingredients
necessary for paradise, certain things that make life
rich and sweet enough to be worth throwing away.

Turning Back

We turn back, always bowing to that urge
to return, to revise, to be certain. What do we want?
Everything we can never get.

Like Orpheus, we turn sharply when we think
we're home free, when we should know better,
when we should know Eurydice's breath

on our backs. What we get is darkness
at the mouth of the cave, the flare of fingertips,
and echoes of *farewell* from the depths.

Like Lot's wife, we become nostalgic.
We remember the salty tinge of warm skin,
the endless nights with the god of desire,

and we have to cast one last longing glance.
What we get is salt in the veins and a footnote
in God's grand book of ironic retribution.

Or like my ancestor Selina, we are defiant,
running back into the house each time
Sherman's troops set a new fire, succeeding

three times before finding flames too large
to overcome. It's February, 1865, and all
this fire won't make it warm. What we get

is watching our convalescent son be carried
out of the house by the Union soldiers
to die quietly on the open mall in a freezing gale.

Let us praise reckless acts, these fierce acts
of futility. Let us always stop, turn back
even when we know that some cold fate,

some heartless soldier, some angry god
will be there, ready to turn us around,
to send us forward, saying *Don't come back.*

Accidents Happen with Clockwork Regularity

For example, when you catch yourself mid-step
and shift your foot aside to avoid crushing
the brilliant green beetle on the sidewalk,
just missing it. The campus bell tower rings noon
in the distance as you stoop for a closer look,
drawn by the insect's metallic sheen. And then you see
that your killing step would have been redundant.
Something has happened, something final.
Already the ants are at their efficient work,
twisting the beetle slowly from side to side
like waves rocking an empty boat. The bells
keep time, twelve dull movements of a slow dance.
Something moves the ants for a while. Something
moves you on. The sky is terribly the same,
full of small engines, birdsong, momentary clouds.
And then you are in your kitchen, cutting onions
at the counter as tears roll from your burning eyes,
waiting for the nightly news while the chicken thaws
in the sink, waiting for the unfortunate accidents
that punctuate the day and night and all the hours
and minutes within, that help you tell time.

Song 246

What song could be in the filthy basement
where the small boy is chained to a beam,

his mouth gagged with an athletic sock?
What song there on this third morning

while his parents keep putting posters of his face
on light poles through the city? What song

could the man sing, the man who lives upstairs,
who comes down four times each day

with enough water to sustain life, lubricant,
and a worn barber's strap? His childlike whimper

when he withdraws could hardly be a song.
Is the cricket singing the glory of the lord

from the dark corner behind the boxes?
Is the light that falls from the high window

onto the cool cement floor a noteless song
to which the scattered roaches dance?

The boy stares and listens. What song could he hear
filtering down through the window from the street?

Could he hear the song blaring from the radio
of the college girl's red convertible while she's stopped

at the traffic light? Could he hear how she loves
this oldies station, loves this old Kool & the Gang song,

loves her car, her sisters, her father's endless money,
and her vague idea of a silent, non-threatening Christ?

Could he hear her hair swaying and her voice singing,
Celebrate good times, come on! along with the radio

as she pulls out and through the intersection before the light
has finished turning green? The boy has never heard that song,

but it's an old favorite of the man, who can't help
humming it as he sharpens the kitchen knife

long after the girl has driven away. Celebrate.
Come on. Hear the song in the basement.

In the boy's ear, percussive footsteps on the stairs
and the crickets' droning hymn that stops and goes.

The Present

My grandmother turns cartwheels in the hall
of the Methodist Home. Mid-morning sunlight
falls through the glass walls. I am ten.

An old woman is turning cartwheels in the hall.
Her hair is thin. She is not my grandmother.
A ten-year-old boy talks to her and smiles.

Outside are the rooks, the thrushes, the nightingales.
Are the leaves and the clouds and the wind.
I am outside, walking the edge of a ditch,

watching crickets and frogs. I am ten.
My grandmother lies in a darkened room
under a soft blanket. She breathes and

breathes again. Today I learn that the cryptomeria
is a timber pine indigenous to Japan. I am thirty-seven.
In Japan, the cryptomeria rise from the earth

for years, grow tall, stand. Bright beetles
crawl up the trees and up the walls of temples,
ornamental jewels that do not remain still. Today

is Respect for the Aged Day in Japan. Today in Alabama
is yesterday in Japan. Today in Japan the trees grow.
A boy is turning cartwheels in the hall.

Day Eight

The lord is embarrassed. He realizes
only now that he will have to inhabit
the world he has made. He will be made
to endure the praises of the thinking creatures
and the indifference of the beautiful ones.
It's going to be hell. It's going to be
day after day of regret and chagrin.
And he wishes he had not made the son
a sacrificial lamb. He wishes he had not
made the daughter's hair auburn.
He wishes he had not left so many questions.
He almost wants to apologize for the mosquito.
It's only morning, but it already feels
like a long day. He's already thinking about the rain.

Still Bound

Still here, and every morning it's almost a surprise
that the sun might come, that it could happen again.
This is how it is. The eagle arrives each day,
but not for my liver. Instead, she comes for my heart.
And it's still agony every time, although I have learned
by now how not to scream. Most days, she lights
on my shoulder, clenching her talons in the flesh,
and right away begins ripping down into my chest,
her head like a cold hammer, tail feathers brushing my nose.
She pulls the heart out in long, thin strips, and flies away,
and I imagine her feeding the dark flesh to her young.
Yet some days, she will light on the rock beside me
and step softly up onto my chest. She will pace along it, stop,
cock her head, and stare into my eyes. Her own dark eye
will bloom wide. She will slowly blink, then lower her beak
to my skin and begin a gentle tearing until her small tongue
is pushing at the shell of my heart. She cuts it out clean
those days and almost seems sorry to leave, to fly off
as my hollowed chest burns. But she does. She flies up
and disappears into the distance, though I can make out
the dwindling speck of her in the great sky for hours.
The day is long. The day is long when you're growing a heart.
Still, look at how the sun falls behind that far peak,
how it glows like one steady eye gazing only here,
how it makes those colors burn and emanate where soon
it will be purely black, how it can make a gift of fire.

What Everything Could Be

Everything must be better than it really is.
A young couple carelessly makes love
on top of their neatly made bed. They find
one clear moment, and afterward they feel
like they are the only animals on earth,
breathing and staring into each other's eyes
in silence. Long minutes pass before she says,
I wonder how long I'll remember this.
He has no answer. Forty years later, she is
dead and the question moot. It must be better.
The ambivalent loons that disappear beneath
the still surface of the lake must invent a world
better than this one in each murky dive,
must become birdfish waving feathered fins
and soaring down toward swimming prey.
Beauty must be a dark world as much as it is
a bright one. Imagine the lines of people
that met in bright sunlight on ancient Attic plains.
Imagine the silence between the lines beforehand
broken by chattering teeth from each phalanx.
Melancholy may very well inhabit the temple
of Delight, the wild West Wind may sound
the trumpet of a prophecy, and I may be
an organic harp. Yet I continue to grow old.
The music of the spheres may be a great symphony
of unbroken silence: void, more void, a crescendo
of void. The pinpricks of light against the black sky
may be the eyes of cold, distant gods. Somewhere
there must be music. Somewhere the lights must be
going out. When I was nine, I told my mother

how I had struck the devil's head while digging
in our backyard, how I had beaten him back to hell
with the shovel's face. *You did? Well, that's good,*
she said, smiling. Then she sent me back outside
to play, to work, to make clouds bloom in the sky,
to watch the ground for sprouting horns and flame.

II

Another Song of the Gods

We live in the darkness, beheld,
    formed in dreams and the heart,
        seen when the light is gone.

We wear the mask of love,
    the mask of desire,
        the red mask of war.

But what are we when the sea
    meets the empty beach
        under the cold stare of the moon?

What are we when we are beheld
    by the small, distant eyes
        of the stars? Are we love?

Are we war? Are we desire?
    Those who call us from the dark
        will not say. They only name us.

Our silent faces, the color of stone,
    stare out steadfastly into the dark,
        empty air. Are we holy?

There is no answer. There is
    no other song. The only song
        is this song.

Our lords make us sing it.
    And then they write it down.
        See how the lords are writing us.

They are wise and mad.
   They sing our lines again and again.
      See how they miraculously die.

Testimony

When the silent Lord turned His back
on my offering and smiled over my brother's
heap of slaughtered lambs, something thick
and warm rose in my throat. I choked it back—
it was not rage that made me take his life.
I grew calm and tried to think, to understand
my God's hard design. I could only reason
that the Lord loved the blood, loved death itself.
For a moment, I even thought of making an offering
of Abel on the very same altar, mixing his blood
with his flock's ashes, spelling out YAHWEH
in the dark muck. But I could imagine judgment,
could see Him turning away again. I remembered then
what mother had said: that He plays with us, planting
the most beautiful trees in the center of our world
and making them forbidden. She said the Fall
was His idea. How could I doubt that now?
In the end, though, it was not anger or thought
that led to this. I simply gave myself up to Him.
When I lifted that sheep's skull to the sky
and brought it down on my brother's head,
I was just being the rough beast that the Lord had made.
My God, my God—He sowed deep that hard seed
of death. I merely reaped its dark red fruit.

The Eve of Ever After

They must have traveled through the night,
covering their heads against the icy storm,
afraid of every sound at their backs, fearing
hyena foemen and older brothers. By morning
they had made it to a small border town
in a safe country. They bought a little house.

Years later, Porphyro sits at the window, dreamily
gazing out, trying to develop an aesthetics
of disappointment. "My heart aches,"
he murmurs, and Madeline glowers
from the basin where she washes his socks.

She often remembers the better times, the early months.
They would spend long mornings in bed, Porphyro
promising to look for work tomorrow. Morning light
would fall across their bodies from the window,
and he would say soft, loving things, none of which
she can remember. She does recall "La Belle Dame,"
but not how he sang it. She remembers the rich trays
of food he would bring her every day that first week
before the price of pomegranates, jellies, and dates
grew too dear. Sometimes, when they thought
they heard one of her father's secret search parties
in the street, they would dart to their hiding place
and muffle their voices with deep kisses, making love
while swords and keys rattled above their heads.

Those were the good times. Before a pale blue sigh
replaced the purple riot in his heart. Before she

lost her figure giving birth to little poets. Long before
the story's end, where every lovely color turns to ash.

Moon Daughter

You smiled when you said you wanted
to name our daughter *Destiny*, our daughter
who does not exist. And you smiled when I
suggested *Chaos* instead. But since she is not

and cannot be, let us make our daughter now
the nameless moon. We could expect her then
to arrive each month, growing from first to full,
fading from last to new, our own daughter

with skin as pale as every evening's light.
At times her pallid face would be obscured,
a perfect stone lying on heaven's riverbed,
washed smooth by a slow current of clouds.

But other times she would be alone in the sky
and would shine, surrounded by her ever-growing hair,
gone from auburn to black, absorbing all light
around her face like everything that never dies.

The Mystery of the Great Blue Heron

The poet tries to make the heron a god,
but the heron does not care. The heron
wades along the shore, a dark body
absorbing light, patience stopping time.
The poet makes sounds like prayer,
but the heron is merely annoyed, stepping
into the air and pulling with broad wings.
The poet carefully records a sacred text,
but the heron has found a hidden pool
among the small trees and stands there
all day, staring coldly into the water,
far from the songs, from the blood,
from all the voices that beg for mercy.

Book of the Father

¹Abraham is with us again. Yeah Abraham, with your God and your son and your rough bone knife. Yeah Abraham, *Geographic* cover boy, father of three faiths, with your Belfast and your Beirut and your Promised Land. ²Yeah Abram to Abraham, patriarch with an extra *ha* dropped in your name. Yeah God's laughter. Yeah Sarah's laughter. Yeah Sarai to Sarah, faux sister to wife. Yeah primal fucking. ³Yeah Abraham, with your needling questions of the Lord. Yeah Abraham, with questions and questions for Lot, but none for Isaac. Yeah knife man. Yeah Abraham, hearing God's voice and turning a murderous eye to a child. Yeah paranoid schizophrenia. ⁴Yeah Abraham, begetting and setting off begetting. Yeah generations of Abraham. Yeah Ibrahim to Ishmael, Abraham to Isaac. Yeah covenant and submission. ⁵Yeah contradictions, one true faith and one true faith. Yeah Abraham, ubiquitous Abraham, everywhere always. In the tank with Ariel Sharon, in the studio with Jerry Falwell, in the cockpit with Mohammed Atta. Yeah Abraham and the small dark fear. Yeah Sodom. Yeah Babel. Yeah down low. ⁶Yeah Abraham and your literal origins. *The father is high.* Yeah the father is high. Yeah Abraham, just like a father, just like a father with a knife. Yeah patriarch, making us all we are. Yeah Abraham. Yeah heavenly father. Yeah testing, loving God. ⁷Yeah.

When the World Was Only Ocean

After the fortieth night of rain, we awoke
to quiet and a great, clear sky. The waves

had already subsided to small ripples
under a bright sun. And by the next dawn,

no ripples, the surface perfectly still.
After a week of silence, we all knew

that we had been forgotten, when the world
was only ocean and the sky empty. None of this

had been about us. The flood was about
what was beneath us. We spent long, still days

looking out over smooth water, afraid
to meet one another's eyes, afraid to speak.

At night, the serpents that filled the lower deck
would begin their incessant hissing. It sounded

like curses in the mouth of God. One morning
the unicorns gave in to despair. They walked to the edge

of the open deck, looked at each other for a moment,
then dropped themselves over the side.

The heavy splash they made filled the day.
We watched them as they sank through water as clear

as the cloudless sky, their large bodies spiraling,
heavy haunches first, their faces staring back up at us.

The points of their horns traced two circles
again and again, all the way down to the silty floor of creation.

Lesson of the Elements: Water

The man wants his water to be pure.
He has been careful not to drink from the tap,
but today he learns that water is always

pre-filtered, each molecule having made its way
through time—through dinosaur, through mastodon,
through urban sewer rat, through everything

that lives. *No new water is ever made on earth,*
says the sign, but the man longs for a fresh drink,
wishes Christ would return to reverse

the world and make him some pure water
out of the finest French wine. He wants
this old world to give him something new.

But Christ will not return, and if He did,
He would only shake the dust of His feet
at the man's doorstep—dust like the dust

that settles in water, making it cloudy
and impure. The man thinks about his head
immersed in water, about holding his breath

until he must inhale. He wonders if he could
take in a deep breath of the water around him
and if that would fill his lungs with purity.

He has to believe such water would be pure
as the water that settled in the lungs of Shelley,
Crane, Woolf, Buckley. He thinks he hears

every sound that's played below the surface—
whale song, echoes of waves on the shore,
notes to accompany the word of the water.

Notes for a Poem in which God Does Not Appear

Assemble materials on a white table.

Images or fragments that form nothing
on Taw Caw Creek, summer 1976.
Drought has hardened the earth enough
to break a shovel. The air is dry, the sky
cloudless. *Do not make the bright sun irony.*
Only let it burn, apart from everything.

Metaphor is the indifferent drone
of the motorboats on the lake, the music
of this world. *Yes.* Metaphor could be
the thin tentacles of memory that entwine
certain hours in certain light. Nothing
on Taw Caw Creek, summer 1976,
but a small, weak boy. *Yes, make him weak.*

But do not try to make his little fists
an emblem of weakness.

Only make them fall on the Collie
to no effect. The indifferent Collie is beauty
clenching its strong, dirty jaws around
the Chihuahua's torso. *What does the Collie feel?*
It does not feel the blows or hear the screams.

And the parents inside do not hear the screams
for a long time. *Make them hear something.*

They hear something. They think it comes

from the television they have left on.
Make them talk on with their guests,
the guests who have brought the Collie.
They hear something or nothing while they talk.
The boy and the dogs. The great sky.

When the parents know what they hear
and rush outside, when the Collie releases
its jaws, the mother falls on the boy
like a blanket on a burning man.

The sky is opened
and opened again.

God should not appear.
He does not.
But if he must,
He does not.
But if he must,
He does not.
But if he must, make him
the Great Father.

The Great Father with his pistol, disappearing
round the corner of the house, following the bright,
torn flesh dragging the ground behind the small dog
that flees, that will hide behind the azaleas
and tremble, licking at its opened side.

And make his majestic voice

His majestic voice is the report that echoes
over the cove's surface and through the pines,

that finally settles in the distant land of small skulls,
dry earth, and trash. In the land of every measured word.

Lost Birds

The birds will not stay. The small, stiff sparrow
is gone, though it was lying on the sidewalk
each morning last week, as cold as the wind on my ears.
A matchbook has lain on the same cement for months,
the word "tattoo" printed in bold black on its red cover.
At the beach, gulls descend, wavering like kites,
to take the bread from my hands at the pier,
watching me with black eyes. Then they float
back up and into the wind like an idea of the soul.
At the lake, the great blue heron stands at the end
of a dock, perfectly still, and then is gone.
The next morning, it is taking slow steps in the reeds
near the shore, twisting time with its patience
before it is gone again. At the quad, a sick robin
watches us from a small tree as we picnic on the grass.
We throw scraps of bread below the tree from our blanket,
and healthy robins descend from the sky,
beat away the weak one, and feast. The sick bird
retreats to the low limbs, looks back at us, and blinks.
And when I am home for a visit, my mother
will complain about the neighbor's stealthy cat
that kills "her birds" near the feeder, catching them
when they scavenge for stray seeds on the ground.
While we're having our coffee, she will tell me
how she found gray feathers strewn below it
just the other morning. She will go to the window
and say, "Oh, there's the dove." And we will stand
together and watch a single bird walk in small circles
on the driveway. She will say, "They usually travel in pairs.
I wonder if that was its mate yesterday. Oh, I *hope* not."

And then I will put my hands on my mother's shoulders,
surprising her, and we will watch the bird walk round
in another small circle and then around again.

Dark Laughter

There's nothing funny about this, she said,
but that only made me laugh harder. I wish
I could have said that inappropriate laughter
is the most human, as is open weeping
after the best sex. *Excess of sorrow laughs,*
said William Blake. *Excess of joy weeps.*
I wish I could have said that we most need
laughter at midnight, surrounded by cold stones.
We need a drunken porter to hold his head,
fart, and make broad jokes about liquor
and cocks while royal blood stains a lady's skin.
Every tragedy calls for a laugh, for a moment
of grinning recognition, a brief nod to the author
of the cosmic comedy. I wish I could have said,
Lighten up, baby. Listen to God's laughter in the night wind.
But I could not catch my breath before she left,
before joy could begin to bring me down.

Corinthians

The old shepherd has died on the return,
and with him, the news. But the people of Corinth
have not given up hope in waiting for their new king.
They have kept a steadfast vigil at the gates, watching
day and night for the shepherd's bald head over the horizon
or even the great clever man himself, come to save them.
Polybus is rotting in the ground. And poor Merope
has died of grief in half a year, mourning for a husband,
yearning for a son. But the people are still waiting,
the snake's hiss of wind through dry grass
playing in their ears. They listen and wait.
They will never believe that he is blind, broken,
not coming. They'll wait and hope for any word at all,
maybe a voice from beyond the hills, maybe a letter
full of good news. They'll wait for their savior forever.

Rhetoric

We want a bastard of a god. [See Hardy's "Hap."]
One to blame for the drought, hurricane, fire, flood.
For the airliner crashing off the coast of Nova Scotia
this morning (all dead). For the blood of the crusades.
For the plan of the Holocaust. For making us like this.
Circumstance, space, and time are never enough.
We want to find higher intent, a god to damn.

But not so. [Ibid.] Not when the cold pinpricks
of starlight argue for distance in the black sky.
Not when the life span of the butterfly underscores
the warrant of time. Not when your father offers
irrefutable evidence: the last days of his grandfather,
rocking in a hallway chair, broken and moaning.
Close the book and look out the window.
See the leaves whirling in the cold rhetoric of the air.

The Egret and the Dawn

The small, bright fish that slowly move
among the reeds and grasses near the shore
receive the dawn slowly. The first light
of the sun seeps into the water from above,

giving shape to the ceiling of their world,
defining the shadows of clouds, trees, dragonflies,
and egrets. The fish feed on what the light gives
near the surface, swimming around the egret's legs.

.

Up early this morning, I walk barefoot out
toward the dock with my coffee, leaving footprints
in the dewy grass. The sun will erase them later
as it burns off the mist that now rises in tendrils

from the glassy surface of the cove. My parents
are asleep, and I think I am alone with the dawn,
but I stop myself halfway to the dock when I see
the great white egret standing in the tall grass

near the shore. The bird seems to be looking
at me, and I look back, trying to remain still
and quiet. But in my stillness and my silence
I am asking this egret to reveal all his secrets

to me, to tell me how the night says nothing,
to show me how time stops with his white movement.
I want to know what the world is when it is only
earth and sea, what the eons say to the sand.

The egret extends his neck, preparing to speak,
and then stabs the water's surface with his long,
sharp beak. He emerges and extends his neck again
to swallow. Without thought, I take three steps

toward the shore before the egret turns his head,
extends his broad wings, and bears himself slowly
over the cove, settling in the grass on the other side.
My mother and father sleep. And I am here, alone

with the dawn, listening to all the smaller birds
begin their songs in the trees. Across the cove, the egret
starts his slow walk near the shore. He has work to do
before the sun pushes another day into the dark.

Song 378

They say that grace is amazing.
They say that fools rush in.
Pope was a wise man. This is a song.

This is a song because it says song,
says song insistently, says sibilance.
Hisses a background for sharp notes.

It says there is a note that marries

skull to smile, despair to hope

if only for one trembling moment.
It sounds the diphthong between birth
and death. This song says mystery.

When the great composer was asked to name
his favorite music, he said, *No music.*
The dead and dying sing a silent song.

The Safe World

You caught yourself when your foot slipped
on the slick porcelain of the bathtub.
You grabbed the safety rail before your temple
could hit the jutting soap dish. And later,
you carelessly dropped your right shoe
before you could get your foot into it,
and the impact with the hardwood floor
ejected the black widow from its dark interior.
And then you spent ten minutes considering
the perfect symmetry of the red hourglass
on the spider's belly. So you arrived
at the intersection ten minutes later
than you otherwise would have, when a bus
plowed through the red light (and two cars),
its driver dead of a massive heart attack
at fifty-two. You are safe, too, from the meteorite
that will strike precisely the same spot later.
That later is not for another hundred
thousand years, when no one will be around
to notice, is immaterial. What's good
is that you won't be at that spot right then.
You'll get to work a little late today.
You'll be held up in traffic, waiting for workers
to clear the wreckage. But you'll be all right.
You'll park in your usual spot near the door.
You'll sit in your comfortable office chair
that smells vaguely like a new car. And before
you begin your first memo, you'll lean back
and look at the sun through large windows.
It will seem almost completely still in the sky

like a Frisbee your dog could always try
to catch. You'll take the time to think
about your grandfather and the German gas,
your father's stumble with the cannon shell,
and the time you were thrown from the motorboat
as its unattended wheel spun hard to the right
and how you watched the boat's widening circles grow
closer to the head you kept above the surface
with treading feet and arms. How the motor
simply died when the fuel line was choked off.
Yes, you're all right today, and today is another day.

Lesson of the Elements: Fire

When he was a young boy, the man
    would light the heads of his plastic army men
        and then become the flame that ate downward,

melting helmet, rifle, canteen, and boots,
    until he was the perfect disc of swirled green
        and black on the driveway pavement.

But tonight he cannot become the flame
    that he starts on the burn ward of the hospital.
        Tonight he can only hear its god-like words.

You could burn it all clean, you know.
    You could make something new out of fresh ash.
        You could be the end and the beginning.

They sound to the man like the voice of God,
    but those words are ours. We say *Ilium* and *auto-da-fé,*
    napalm and *Nagasaki.* Our words are like tongues

of flame atop toy soldiers, consuming us as soon
    as we utter them. We speak swirls of fiery stars
        back at the cosmos. Our words make flames rise

like the screams of victims or like the body
    of a god ascending into heaven. We say
        Alpha and *Omega,* one and another word of the fire.

III

The Last Song of the One True God

The last song of the one true god
is silent because the one true god
sings in a vacuum behind the thick,
black wall. Ideas of notes rise and fall
like shadows on a flat screen. Listen.
Nothing can be heard. It's like
the mumbled prayers of the prophet
in the wilderness, that sound
that falls on sand and sinks.
No one hears. It's like the sound
of the Indian earthquake, the sound
no one can describe now amidst
the hundred thousand dead, one week
after thirty million bathed in the Ganges.
Listen to the one true god sing.
It's like the tiny white flowers that bloom
on the head of the Korean Buddha,
each one a bright, discrete note
in the song none of us will ever hear.

All the Birds in Unison

A boy is screaming in the driveway.
He puts his small hands to his head
and pulls them away to see the blood.
A crow takes halting steps across the lawn,
black enough to swallow sound and light.
The azaleas are blooming, and above,
one large eye masquerades as a cloud.
When the boy's older sisters run to him
and the Brittany spaniel begins to bark,
the crow lazily flies to a low tree limb.
When the family car pulls into the road,
all the birds in unison lift themselves
out of the tree, rise and bank away
like one black ghost, leaving everything
bright and bare under the dissipating clouds.

Methuselah Dead

After all that forestallment, still this. Methuselah
in the ground, and even then with great company,
with Mahalaleel, Jared, and Enoch, whom God took.
Poor Enoch, at only three hundred and sixty-five.
No more sun or sky, nor the lush green or brilliant sand.
Earth was growing crowded, above and below. No more
fathering sons at one hundred and eighty-seven, nor
after. Cainan, Enos, Seth. And the women. My God,
the women, so fair. There will be no more naming
of beasts, no smiles, no coaxing. It is all too much.
And even Adam himself with his damned smooth belly.
Methuselah, who had put this off for so long, is pressed
up against him by the crowd, the packed earth,
the encroaching roots. Uncomfortable proximity,
and too much bitterness for an old man to swallow,
cracked lips to father's ear: *This is all your fault.*

What Else Means Death

What images return
O my daughter.
                    —Eliot

Flowers blooming in the stone fields, glinting
bits of shell in fine sand, the regular tide, stars
flaring in the millennial distance, regret and time,
the last page of a short novel, the hard ground
behind dumpsters, trilobites, wedding days,
splinters and cells, words from the holy text,
winter air, fathers as old as their own fathers,
satin lining, the sharp venom of insects, smiles
deeper than flesh, line after line, any sharpened
tooth, any daughter, any goddamned marina.

Exeunt

When you think about it, the English ambassadors
make remarkable time, following their king's
efficient dispatch of royal orders. Blink an eye,
and they are here, bouncing onto stage to say,
Rosencrantz and Guildenstern are dead, and collect.
But they are always late. Always late, every time.
Ophelia is bloated, and her father rots. Hamlet
and Laertes have nicked each other. The queen
has swallowed and spilt red wine down the front
of her beautiful gown. Claudius himself has taken
the sword and a final draught. This is how it ends.
The living look at each other and murmur.
Outside the clouds drift by, looking like camels,
whales, and clouds. Fortinbras has his moment,
and the band strikes up a dead march. Actors
follow their cues. Then the sun sets, the curtain
falls, and it's all black. There is nothing to see.
The littered stage seems empty, everything silent.

In the Era of the Sentence Fragment

Lines of incompletion. All those words
that can be gathered. But not enough
for shoring. Not against ruins. Fragments
of sentences, of dreams, of the boys' school
in Hiroshima. Looking for raw material
in the dust. Finding nothing. Having nothing
inside. Unable to do the police in different voices.
No more voices. No more makers, better
or worse. Only weak echoes. And irony.
And the dim blue sunrise of the television screen.
And the wish finally to die, like Shelley,
mid-sentence. Writing the triumph of life.

The Maenads

She is the one who can redeem you. See her
there, standing next to the punch bowl,
with her hair pulled tight. Watch her stare
with narrowed eyes, see how she draws her lips thin.
Your world lies deep beneath her contempt.
But give her wine and the wilderness, give her
open space and the free air, and watch her fill
with the spirit of the wood. She will ignite
like the silent explosion of a remote star. See her
eyes glow, her hair float loose like visible wind.
Listen to her voice rise in the sharp darkness.
It takes the hand of a god to form such rough beauty.
What will you give her? What could you offer?
She wants *the joy of the blood and the raw red flesh.*
She will tear through Pentheus, through Orpheus,
through all of us. The blood of all our fathers
drips from her bared teeth. But you must try
to kiss her, to touch her full red lips. Try to hold
what trembles through her. Try to make yourself real.
Clasp her hand and join this dark worship.
Listen to the night air in the trees, the rasp of her holy
breath, the movement of blood through your veins.
Let it happen. Let there be life and death.

Lesson of the Elements: Earth

And when the rains came, the people there
could not tell dust from ash from clay. They could not
distinguish what was of the earth or of the ocean.
Nor of the air or of the flame. We could tell them
that we are all of the flame, composed of the stuff
of ever-burning stars. That we are of the water,
more than two-thirds water. That we are of the air,
respiring spirits. That we are of the earth, from dust
to dust. But none of that would give them comfort.
Our answers are no better than Horatio's
to Hamlet in the graveyard. *E'en so, my lord.*
We stand on the rock that is only the rock
and the dirt and the flesh. We stand on an old world
that is handful after handful of dust. In fear,
the woman taken in the act of adultery—*the very act,*
O lord—stood on this earth before her accusers.
Christ wrote in the sand and she lived.
But the day before or after, was there not
another woman in that same circle of men?
Think of her—younger, prettier, a girl, really—
with only smiles for her judges. Think of the first stone
catching her square in the eye. That one puts her down
and makes it easier for the rest of the men to pour
their heavy pieces of earth onto her prostrate form.
Think of the stone in each man's hand with the heft of sin.
Think of the young woman's last vision of this world,
its dusty floor growing darker, each stone pressing her
harder against it, the friction of her face on the grainy sand
making the whispered word of the earth.

Song 437

The resonant bass notes of the organ swirling together
in a chaotic rise between the third and fourth verses
of the hymn. The boy's skull found in the wooded field.
Imagined souls floating. Paolo and Francesca together
forever in a small tempest. A brief wind through trees.
There is one perfectly useless expletive sentence
full of cadence that everyone hears in a wordless language.
Still, the searching. His hands and her lips.
Their movement together, another attempt.
The failure of the soprano to move in her stillness.
A swimmer in trouble whose voice mingles
with the waves. Not waving, nor drowning. Dancing.

Things to Do in the Belly of the Whale

Measure the walls. Count the ribs. Notch the long days.
Look up for blue sky through the spout. Make small fires
with the broken hulls of fishing boats. Practice smoke signals.
Call old friends, and listen for echoes of distant voices.
Organize your calendar. Dream of the beach. Look each way
for the dim glow of light. Work on your reports. Review
each of your life's ten million choices. Endure moments
of self-loathing. Find the evidence of those before you.
Destroy it. Try to be very quiet, and listen for the sound
of gears and moving water. Listen for the sound of your heart.
Be thankful that you are here, swallowed with all hope,
where you can rest and wait. Be nostalgic. Think of all
the things you did and could have done. Remember
treading water in the center of the still night sea, your toes
pointing again and again down, down into the black depths.

Stones and Shadows

1. Visiting the Stone

The air in the car is thick and still. My father makes
a right turn through the cemetery gates, giving me
a significant look. I don't ask why. "The mausoleum
keeps expanding," he says, without irony.

"Have you ever been to a *filing*? Your mother and I
went to our first last week." I give him the short laugh
that he knows well. Not funny yet again. But I see
that he's right—the mausoleum *is* expanding.

Construction materials are stacked nearby, and the frame
of an addition has been erected. The original building
is crowded. White flowers adorn its smooth stone wall
in odd spots as if they had been thrown against it

at random. We step out of the car at the back
of the graveyard, and my father leads me
to a new headstone. Then he gestures to the ten letters
cut into its face, shadows hiding in the furrows.

He tells me he likes the view and how important
that is when you think about spending eternity
in one place. Small birds stand like sentinels
on the neighboring monuments, watching us

with black pearls of eyes. Like the stone angels,
they keep us under constant vigil. Low clouds
drift by. The sound of traffic from the highway
is insufferable. I smile at my father and try

to think of kind things to say to him. He smiles.
But driving home, he is again the man I know.
"How would you like to live on Dargan Street?"
he asks with contempt as we pass the beaten houses

of the poor. "How would you like to live
in New York City?" I search for ways to interrupt,
to shut him up. But when I look left, he has become
just a voice in the driver's seat. "Son," says the voice.

"Son, I think it's going to be a good year for you."
The car arrives at the house, where my mother
is waiting, asking where we've been. She holds
the door open for us—me, the voice, my father's body.

2. Shadow

In the late afternoon, he is cooking steaks on the grill,
and we're drinking beer. The clouds have moved on.
Purple martins dart across the air, catching mosquitoes
and going in and out of their houses. We are privileged

in the extreme. And I don't want this to be a poem
of complaint. I only want to say that my father and I
are quiet. That there are words necessary and impossible,
words as grand as shadows cast by stones.

He stabs at a steak with his fork and says, "This one
is your mother's—she doesn't want any blood in hers.
She wants it about as well done as done can be."
My mother's in the kitchen, cooking the potatoes.

The shadows of the martins swim in the grass.
The shadows of the grass dig into the earth.
The shadows of the earth carve the moon
into crescents, halves, and empty holes.

I notice that the sundial in the plant bed is not
positioned well. "Your sundial is keeping bad time,"
I tell my father. He smiles and says, "That's not
what I got it for," pointing to the image in relief,

old man with scythe, and the quotation: "Grow old
along with me, the best is yet to be." Impossible,
grand. The earth is beneath us. The birds watch us.
The blade's shadow quietly cuts X from I.

Poem in which God Does Not Appear

The earth hard from months of drought, the pines
with stiff needles, the water moccasins in the reeds.
Oh my lord, my God. The drone of outboard motors
carried over the water, the slap of small waves
on the boats' sides, the sounds that dogs and boys
can make. *Oh my lord, my God.* The sky becoming
everything beneath it, blood black against a dark shirt,
the mother's heart, the mother's beating heart. *Oh my lord,*
my God. The father's steel eye and iron soul, the sky,
the night swallowing every star. *Oh my lord, my absent God.*

Revision

After two weeks under the Italian sun,
he would dash off a note to Fanny Brawne:
"Weather marvelous. Fully recovered.
Come soon and bring summer dresses."
And she would come. She would pull
his miraculous heart to her breast,
and they would listen to every bird's song.
The odes would win a silly contest,
and they would use the prize money
to build a small house on a Greek island.
They would spend the next twenty years
perfecting the art of the human body.
They would eat fine olives and swallow
the sound of each wave's roll onto the beach.
They would make love under the night sky
with such tense clarity that the moon
would become the bright face of God.
One morning the man would pick up his pen,
sit by the window, write, "I was happy
to be John Keats," and never write again.

The Boatloads

Dante had not thought death had undone so many.
He had not been paying attention. Just look
at the front page every morning, its solid column
of names. It looks like the print of a rubber stamp,
rough from reuse. At the bank of the river,
hoary old Charon can barely keep up.
Each day he has more trips to make,
each day a longer list, the sheet curling
at his toes. Back for another load, he moors
his boat and begins calling out, *Adam, Mary,*
Sarah, Thomas, running down the roll.
But before he's halfway through, there's pushing
at the back of the line and no relief in sight.
In the end, Charon must abandon formality,
must drop the roll, extend his bony finger
toward the crowd, and begin counting off,
you and you, and *you and you and you.*

Acknowledgments

I offer grateful acknowledgment to the editors of the publications in which the following poems, some in slightly different forms, first appeared:

Ascent: "Methuselah Dead" and "The Safe World"
Asheville Poetry Review: "The Maenads"
Backwards City Review: "Book of the Father"
Borderlands: Texas Poetry Review: "Lesson of the Elements: Fire" and "What Everything Could Be"
Cave Wall: "Lost Birds" and "Song 378"
The Distillery: "Among the Things He Does Not Deserve" and "The Mystery of the Great Blue Heron"
Ecotone: "Day Eight" and "A Prayer for My Daughter, Who Does Not Exist"
The Greensboro Review: "Stones and Shadows"
The Laurel Review: "The Age of Adam"
Meridian: "What Else Means Death"
Mid-American Review: "Accidents Happen with Clockwork Regularity," "Lesson of the Elements: Earth," and "Thumbs"
Natural Bridge: "Testimony" and "When the World Was Only Ocean"
New Orleans Review: "In the Era of the Sentence Fragment"
Poem: "Song of the Gods"
Prairie Schooner: "Turning Back"
Shenandoah: "Lesson of the Elements: Air"
The Southeast Review: "Bad Language" and "Exeunt"
Southern Humanities Review: "All the Birds in Unison," "The Egret and the Dawn," "The Eve of Ever After," "The Osprey and the Late Afternoon," and "Things to Do in the Belly of the Whale"

The Southern Review: "The Chiming of the Hour" and "Moon
  Daughter"
Tar River Poetry: "The Present"
The Virginia Quarterly Review: "Revision"

"Stones and Shadows" was reprinted in *Best New Poets 2005,*
  edited by George Garrett.
"Things to Do in the Belly of the Whale" won the 2005 Oneiros
  Press Poetry Broadside Contest.
"The Osprey and the Late Afternoon" won the 1999 Theodore
  Christian Hoepfner Award from *Southern Humanities Review.*

Several of the poems in this collection also appeared in the lim-
ited edition chapbook *Charon's Manifest,* published by the North
Carolina Writers' Network in 2005.

I also wish to thank the Bread Loaf Writers' Conference, the
Sewanee Writers' Conference, and the Virginia Center for the
Creative Arts for scholarships and fellowships that supported the
conception, drafting, and revision of many of these poems.

I owe great debts to my teachers for their insights, guidance, and
encouragement: Fred Chappell, Stuart Dischell, Christine Garren,
Alan Shapiro, and Natasha Trethewey. And in memoriam, James
Dickey.

Finally, I wish to thank Edward Hirsch for selecting my manu-
script for the A. Poulin, Jr. Poetry Prize and Thom Ward, Peter
Conners, Nora Jones, and everyone at BOA Editions for their
help and support.

About the Author

Dan Albergotti's poems have appeared in *The Cincinnati Review, Shenandoah, The Southern Review, The Virginia Quarterly Review,* and other journals. He has been a scholar at the Sewanee and Bread Loaf writers' conferences and a fellow at the Virginia Center for the Creative Arts. A graduate of the MFA program at UNC Greensboro and former poetry editor of *The Greensboro Review,* he currently serves as Coordinator of Creative Writing at Coastal Carolina University in Conway, SC, where he teaches creative writing and literature courses.

BOA Editions, Ltd.
The A. Poulin, Jr. New Poets of America Series

No. 1 *Cedarhome*
Poems by Barton Sutter
Foreword by W. D. Snodgrass

No. 2 *Beast Is a Wolf with Brown Fire*
Poems by Barry Wallenstein
Foreword by M. L. Rosenthal

No. 3 *Along the Dark Shore*
Poems by Edward Byrne
Foreword by John Ashbery

No. 4 *Anchor Dragging*
Poems by Anthony Piccione
Foreword by Archibald MacLeish

No. 5 *Eggs in the Lake*
Poems by Daniela Gioseffi
Foreword by John Logan

No. 6 *Moving the House*
Poems by Ingrid Wendt
Foreword by William Stafford

No. 7 *Whomp and Moonshiver*
Poems by Thomas Whitbread
Foreword by Richard Wilbur

No. 8 *Where We Live*
Poems by Peter Makuck
Foreword by Louis Simpson

No. 9 *Rose*
Poems by Li-Young Lee
Foreword by Gerald Stern

No. 10 *Genesis*
Poems by Emanuel di Pasquale
Foreword by X. J. Kennedy

No. 11 *Borders*
Poems by Mary Crow
Foreword by David Ignatow

No. 12 *Awake*
Poems by Dorianne Laux
Foreword by Philip Levine

No. 13 *Hurricane Walk*
Poems by Diann Blakely Shoaf
Foreword by William Matthews

No. 14 *The Philosopher's Club*
Poems by Kim Addonizio
Foreword by Gerald Stern

No. 15 *Bell 8*
Poems by Rick Lyon
Foreword by C. K. Williams

No. 16 *Bruise Theory*
Poems by Natalie Kenvin
Foreword by Carolyn Forché

No. 17 *Shattering Air*
Poems by David Biespiel
Foreword by Stanley Plumly

No. 18 *The Hour Between Dog and Wolf*
Poems by Laure-Anne Bosselaar
Foreword by Charles Simic

No. 19 *News of Home*
Poems by Debra Kang Dean
Foreword by Colette Inez

No. 20 *Meteorology*
Poems by Alpay Ulku
Foreword by Yusef Komunyakaa

No. 21 *The Daughters of Discordia*
Poems by Suzanne Owens
Foreword by Denise Duhamel

No. 22 *Rare Earths*
Poems by Deena Linett
Foreword by Molly Peacock

No. 23 *An Unkindness of Ravens*
Poems by Meg Kearney
Foreword by Donald Hall

No. 24 *Hunting Down the Monk*
Poems by Adrie Kusserow
Foreword by Karen Swenson

No. 25 *Big Back Yard*
Poems by Michael Teig
Foreword by Stephen Dobyns

No. 26 *Elegy with a Glass of Whiskey*
Poems by Crystal Bacon
Foreword by Stephen Dunn

Colophon

The Boatloads by Dan Albergotti is set in Minion by Scott McCarney, Rochester, New York. The cover design is by Geri McCormick. The cover art, *Chairs*, by Anne Havens, is courtesy of the artist. Manufacturing was by Thomson-Shore.

The publication of this book is made possible in part by the special support of the following individuals:

Anonymous (2)
Alan & Nancy Cameros
Gwen & Gary Conners
Peter & Sue Durant
Pete & Bev French
Dane & Judy Gordon
Kip & Debby Hale
Tom & Illona Hansen
Stephen Healey, in honor of Myrna MacPhail
Peter & Robin Hursh
Willy & Bob Hursh
X. J. & Dorothy M. Kennedy
Jack & Gail Langerak
Rosemary & Lewis Lloyd
Peter & Phyllis Makuck
Robert & Francie Marx
Boo Poulin
Steven O. Russell & Phyllis Rifkin-Russell
Jane Moress Schuster
Vicki & Richard Schwartz
Joseph Shields & Patti Hall
Barbara Valente & Thom Ward
Patricia D. Ward-Baker
Dan & Nan Westervelt
Pat & Mike Wilder
Glenn & Helen William
Steven & Erica Yunghans